I Invited a Dragon to Dinner

and Other Poems to Make You
Laugh Out Loud

illustrated by

CHRIS L. DEMAREST

Philomel Books • New York

Mouse House

MARY CIOTKOWSKI

One mouse moved into my house.
I did not mind.
I let him stay but now I find . . .

His mother's in the parlor
And his father's on the stair.
His sister's in the pantry
And his brother's in my chair.
His grandma's in the closet
While his grandpa climbs the drapes.
His uncle's in the kitchen
Eating sausages and grapes.
His aunts are in my dresser
Making nests among my socks
And his cousins ate the workings
Of my radios and clocks!
I cannot even count them.
There are more and more each day.
If they keep on moving in,
I shall have to move away!

I Invited a Dragon to Dinner

DAVE CRAWLEY

I invited a dragon to dinner.
My parents were really surprised.
They thought he would wish for lobster and fish,
But he ordered a burger and fries.

Since he was lacking in fingers,
He scooped up his food with his paws.
The napkin was hapless since dragons are lapless.
It merely got stuck in his claws.

Though his manners were clearly abysmal,
The dragon showed no sign of shame.
And each time he spoke he billowed with smoke,
While his mouth erupted in flame.

Dessert was a bucket of ice cream,
And juice he was eager to quaff.
With one final slurp and a dragon-sized burp,
He said, "Well, I guess I'll be off."

The lessons I learned were winners,
As he flew away with a squawk.
Don't invite dragons to dinner.
And don't get too close when they talk!

The Human Pickle

DENISE LONG

There once was a girl
Named A. K.,
Who loved to eat pickles
All day.

Two in the morning,
Three for a snack,
Five more at lunch,
All back-to-back.

Eight more for dinner,
One for dessert,
One would have thought
That her body would hurt.

But she just couldn't quit.
She kept right on going—
Her pickle intake
Just wasn't slowing.

When her pee turned green
Her folks were unnerved.
She was put in a jar
So that she'd be preserved.

And thanks to her brother,
For only a nickel,
We can all view her—
The first human pickle.

My Mother Has Gone Crazy

SUZANNE WUNDER

My mother has gone crazy.
I think she's lost her head.
She toasted all my socks,
And she washed a loaf of bread.
She put jelly on my toothbrush
And said, "Scrub between your toes."
Then she gave me her best tablecloth
And said, "Here, blow your nose."
She put my little sister
In the yard and told the cat,
"Don't go out unless you're wearing
Some mittens and a hat."
She kissed the dog good-bye two times,
And told my dad to stay.
My mother has gone crazy but . . .
I like my mom this way.

The Attic

DAVE CRAWLEY

There's a rumble in the attic.
A grumble in the attic.
I fear I hear (it's very clear)
A stumble in the attic.
It sounds a bit dramatic,
But I can't be more emphatic:
Something, with a mumble,
Took a tumble in the attic.

I hear a loud ka-thumping.
Rhinoceroses bumping?
Or kangaroos with heavy shoes?
Could elephants be jumping?
I hear it through the ceiling.
Alligators squealing.
While prancing pigs are dancing jigs
And walruses are wheeling.

I climbed the attic ladder
To see what was the matter.
And then I grinned. It's just the wind
That made that noisy clatter!
The window needs replacement.
I'll close the attic casement.
But now it's clear, I fear I hear
A babble in the basement!

Under the Bed

PENNY TRZYNKA

There's a terrible green monster
    Who lives beneath my bed.
I hear his long white teeth click.
    He's waiting to be fed.
I shiver underneath my sheets
    And squeeze my eyes up tight.
Maybe if I lie real still
    He won't eat me tonight. . . .
He taps me on the shoulder.
    I don't know what to do.
He looks at me and says, "I'm scared!
    Can I get in with you?"

The Man in the Green Hat That No One Can See

B. H. FIELDS

Down on the ceiling, up on the floor,
Inside the walls, and outside the door,
That's where I'll find him, that's where he'll be,
The man in the green hat that no one can see.

He might wear a red hat, or yellow, or blue.
They're as bright as the green and invisible, too.
But he wears the green so I know that it's he
When I'm looking at someone that no one can see.

He shouts in a loud voice that no one can hear,
So I won't knock him over by coming too near,
And his best aftershave suits him ever so well,
For it has a fine fragrance that no one can smell.

He bakes scrumptious cookies that no one can taste,
And he shares them with me so they won't go to waste.
But we don't eat too many. We won't spoil our meal
With an "ouch" of a bellyache no one can feel.

You never can tell where you'll find him yourself,
On the roof, in the basement, or up on the shelf.
When you find him, his hat may be purple or blue,
'Cause no one imagines exactly like you.

Theodore Standitch

Penny Trzynka

Theodore Standitch built a sandwich
    One sunny summer day.
He began with bread and toenail spread
    Then sprinkled it with hay.
A can of Spam, a candied yam,
    A red worm from the ground;
Canned sardines and jelly beans,
    A dirty sock he found.
Kids came down and stood around
    To watch the sandwich grow.
He added wires and threw on tires.
    He put on quite a show.
Then Theodore ate it, all but the plate.
    He chewed and chomped and slurped.
Said he, "I'm done! That was such great fun!"
    And he gave a tremendous burp.

Billy Bupper

ROBERT ORA THOMAS

Billy Bupper likes to eat,
He also likes to play,
And so to save a little time
He dresses up this way:
With bologna in his pockets,
And cheese between his toes,
A tomato slice behind each ear,
And pickles up his nose,
An onion tucked beneath his chin,
And mustard in his hair,
Three leaves of crispy lettuce
Hidden in his underwear.
And underneath each armpit
A slice of bread is scrunched,
So when Billy does a somersault
He also makes his lunch.

Martin's Extra Energy

LISA KLIEFOTH

As Martin bounced from bed to bed
His poor exhausted mother said,
"It occurs to me your kilowatt
Is burning just a bit too hot."
She tied a key around his nose
And hooked it to a metal hose.
She looped the hose around a switcher
Then fed it through a pewter pitcher

She ran it up a metal pole,
Through the ceiling, through a hole,
Across the roof, a hundred feet,
Down the block and down the street,
Through the city, post to post,
Up and down the whole East Coast.
And when she flipped a little switch,
The system worked without a hitch.
From Boston south, the lights burned bright.
She tucked him in, and said "Good night."
And to this day, on normal power,
He makes three cents per kilowatt hour.

The Invitation

DORIAN CIRRONE

So Caitlin didn't send me one.
Big deal. Who cares? Not me.
I never liked her anyway.
She's not my cup of tea.
Her hair's too short, she laughs too loud,
She wears her pants too long.
And when the teacher calls on her,
She always answers wrong.

Who cares about her birthday bash,
The games that she has planned?
Oh, no. She's walking over here.
There's something in her hand.
"I found this in my room at home.
I hope that you can come.
I meant to hand it out to you
With all the other ones."

"Oh sure," I say, "I'd love to come.
It's late. So what. That's fine."
You know, that Caitlin's always been
A favorite friend of mine.

Show Time

EILEEN SHERIDAN

Who's that on the stage before us,
Doing high kicks with the chorus?
Why, it's the tyrannosaurus!
Watch that dino soar!
Who'd have thought he'd be so sprightly,
Landing on his feet so lightly?
Will he be appearing nightly?
How strong is the floor?

Flee Flea

FONDA BELL MILLER

Our cats have fleas
And we have spray.
There's just one flea
That got away,

And it's inside
oo—HOO!—my pants!
So, please excuse
This flee flea dance.

Why Do I Have to Be Clean?

JUDY DYL

Do tarantulas shampoo the hair on their legs?
Does a prairie dog polish his teeth?
Does a bat wipe his fangs before dining on bugs,
Making sure that they're clean underneath?

Does a toad lick her warts till they gleam in the sun?
Does an inchworm shrug off clinging dust?
Does a snake slither out for an afternoon scrub
Just to keep all his scales free of rust?

Do mosquitoes prick soap suds to wash out their mouths?
Does a jackrabbit swab out his ears?
Does a ladybug try to scrub off her black spots?
When she can't, does she burst into tears?

Does a centipede bathe all his legs in a pond,
A woodpecker pick wood from his beak?
Does a porcupine comb out her quills in neat rows?
Does a skunk need to clean up her reek?

All those creatures are happy. They live with their dirt.
But I soak and I lather and scrub.
My mean mom makes me clean every corner of me,
And then makes me wipe out the tub!

Time Out

WENDI SILVANO

The shoe I hit my sister with was rubbery and soft.
And the chewed-up crackers on the floor went spraying when I coughed.
I know the couch is smelly, but that's just the way with trout.
Could someone please explain to me . . . why am I in time out?
There's good reason why the kitchen wall is splattered with red paint.
And why the blender's broken . . . I can't always be a saint.
And if you'll let me I'll explain what this hole is all about.
But could someone please explain to *me* . . . why am I in time out?
I did put glue in Father's shoe, but try to understand.
The project I was working on was something truly grand.
And midnight's not so bad an hour to scream and yell and shout.
Could someone please explain to me . . . why am I in time out?
So I shared Mom's hairbrush with the dog. Isn't sharing good?
And I cut Dad's tie down to his size just as any good kid would.
I try to be the best I can, but it never does work out.
Could someone PLEASE explain to me . . . why am I in time out?

Detestable Vegetables

Jason Hunt

Detestable vegetables,
Vile and inedible—
These are the foods that I hate.
I wouldn't even wanna
Subject an iguana
To some of this stuff on my plate!
Okra can choke ya,
And barley is gnarly,
And Popeye can keep all that spinach.
My mama's a meanie
To make me zucchini
And think that I might even finish.
Onions are terrible,
Carrots, unbearable,
Tomatoes I hate most of all.
Lima beans, kidney beans,
Red, white and pinto beans
Ought to be thrown at the wall.
Peas, in particular,
Make me feel sicklier—
Even my dad makes a face.
But let Mama frown,
And he eats them all down
Without even pleading his case.
Maybe I'm picky,
But eggplant is icky.
I have to say, "No, thank you, ma'am."
I know I'll get thinner,
But can't we skip dinner?
I'd rather read *Green Eggs and Ham*.

Ice Cream on the Side

ELIZABETH DESCHRYVER

When I grow up, I'm going to run
A giant restaurant.
I'll be the chef, and get to cook
Just anything I want.

I'll scramble eggs with butterscotch,
And pile pancakes high,
With chocolate syrup, applesauce,
And ice cream on the side.

I'll make a popcorn-pickle cake,
And bake bologna pie,
With crunchy peanut butter crust
And ice cream on the side.

I'll serve spaghetti seven ways,
Baked and boiled and fried,
Stirred and stewed and fricasseed,
And ice cream on the side.

My fame will spread for miles around,
They'll come from far and wide.
I'll give them all a big, big smile—
With ice cream on the side.

Another Rainy Day

SUSAN MAREE JEAVONS

I'm feeling quite froggy
'Cause the ground is so soggy.
It has rained every day for a week!
My skin's turning green,
Flies look yummy to me,
And I'm starting to croak when I speak!
Oh, I wish it would stop!
All I do now is hop!
This rain doesn't make any sense!
On the bright side of this,
If you give me a kiss,
I might just turn into a prince!

A New View

JILL ESBAUM

Susie dropped her glasses
In the mud beside the brook.
Now everybody Susie meets
Gets a dirty look.

The Tickle

EILEEN SHERIDAN

There's a little tickle starting
Way down deep inside my toes.
Soon that tickle will be looking
For a way to reach my nose.
It will slide up to my ankles.
It will jump into my knees.
It will buzz my belly button
Like a swarm of angry bees.
It will leap onto my shoulder
Or land lightly on my chin,
And the minute my mouth opens,
That old tickle will rush in.
It will latch onto my tonsils
Just to make me cough and wheeze.
It will do a double back flip,
Hit my nose and make me sneeze.
Now that sneeze might be a small one,
Hardly any sneeze at all,
But it might be so gigantic
That it makes the ceiling fall!
I can feel that tickle moving. . . .
Is there anyone who knows
How to stop a little tickle
That's been growing in your toes?

Sister Sally

ROXANNE M. KINNE

My sister Sally swallowed a squirrel,
Which was a pretty good trick for a girl.
Now Sally eats peanuts and chatters all day,
But she did that before, so no one can say
If the squirrel she gulped down changed her at all—
Except now she climbs trees and stores nuts in the fall.

Zoops!

PAT L. SIMONS

Octopus and rhinoceros fell in love one day
And made a little Rhino-pus who grew and moved away.
Rhino-pus then made a fuss about a big baboon,
And they gave birth (for what it's worth) to Rhino-bus-o-poon.
When she became the blushing bride of pompous parakeet,
These two made (in an egg she laid) Rhi-bus-o-poon-o-tweet.
This most peculiar creature adored a honeybee,
And they produced (inside their roost) the Poon-o-rhi-bus-hee,
A mixed-up mingle-mangle who wed a kangaroo,
Who then gave birth (right on this earth!) to a
Swimming
stalking
swinging
squawking
stinging
springing
zoo!

Thoughts I Was Thinking While Drinking My Juice

Dave Crawley

I was thinking this morning, while drinking my juice,
That it's quite easy telling a moose from a goose.
A goose doesn't gallop. There's no need to try.
And whoever heard of a moose that could fly?

The moose is a mammal. The goose is a bird.
A goose joins a gaggle. The moose has a herd.
But what do I call them? What's the right use
Of a name to describe more than one goose or moose?

I pour some more juice. I now have two juices.
But never, not ever, could I have two mooses.
Two gooses? Of course not! That just isn't done!
It does get confusing to have more than one!

It is proper to talk about seventeen geese,
But nobody ever had forty-one meese.
If there should be more than one moose on the loose,
The name is the same. There are sixty-two moose.

But I wonder, whatever could be the right words
For more than one gaggle, or eighty-one herds?
Is it gooses and moose, or geeses and mooses?
I don't really care. I've finished my juices.

Catching Cold

ELIZABETH DESCHRYVER

Mama says I caught a cold.
I wonder how I caught it?
I didn't use a fishing pole,
Or hook or line to bait it.

I didn't throw a big harpoon
To spear it like a whale,
I didn't use a lariat
To rope it on the trail.

I didn't snare it with a net,
Or bag it in a sack,
I didn't jump it in the dark
While playing sneak attack.

I didn't use a baseball glove
To catch it on the fly,
I didn't jump, or dive, or roll—
I didn't even try.

Now all I do is sniff and sneeze
And cough and wheeze and hack.
Oh, I don't care how I caught it—
I'd like to throw it back!

Maximillian's Mouth

TED SCHEU

You hear it comin' down the tracks.
But there's no way to stop the mouth of Max.
Don't stand in its way, you'll be run over flat.
It's comin' through, and that is that.

Max-i-mil-lian, Max-i-mil-lian,
Mum-bling, Rum-bling,
Yelling, Swelling,
Chittering, Chattering,
Jibbering, Jabbering,
Clittering, Clattering,
Jawing, Cawing,
Finding flawing,
Teasing, Wheezing,
Never pleasing,
Yakety yakking,
Talking backing,
Can't you seeing,
Call on meing,
Me first! Me first!
Outburst! Outburst!
Inter-rup-tion!
Inter-rup-tion!

The train eventually goes away
When Max and his mouth go home for the day.
The peace that comes when that occurs
Makes ears grin broadly, mine and yours.

Closet

FONDA BELL MILLER

I organized my closet,
It's now a better place.
I organized my closet
And each shoe has a space.

"You know where all your stuff is!"
My mother proudly said.
I do know where my stuff is.
(It's underneath my bed.)

Coming Unscrewed

CLAUDIA HARRINGTON

There once was a lady who took off her head
Because all her toes stuck out of her bed.
She simply unscrewed it, decided to venture
To put it beside her, right next to her dentures.
And there it would sit, with a blink or a yawn,
From the time she dozed off until just after dawn.

Bedtime Prayer

ANDREA PERRY

Deliver me, Lord, from big bullies named Ned,
From mushrooms, and spinach, and making my bed,
From tests, and from homework, from gum on my shoe,
From splinters, and bee stings, and food I can't chew.

Shield me from sunburn, from cleaning up toys,
From stepping on nails, and thunderstorm noise.
Spare me the measles. Please keep me from snakes,
And stitches, and head lice, and painful earaches.

Protect me from dog bites, from Limburger cheese,
From hiccups, retainers, and kites stuck in trees.
Guard me against getting holes in my socks,
Soap in my eyes, and big red chicken pox.

Deliver me, Lord, from cheek-pinching Aunt Sue,
From smelling the elephant cage at the zoo,
From car sickness, blisters, and cold sores, and then,
Don't forget liver and onions. Amen.

Cosmic Cafe

KATHY DUVAL

If the moon is made of cheese,
Give me one thick moon slice, please.
Put it on a rainbow bun,
Melt it in the setting sun;
Add a dash of twilight stars
And a splash of bright red Mars—
A moon sandwich to end the day
Before I drink my Milky Way.

MARY CIOTKOWSKI has loved to write and draw for as long as she can remember. It all came together for her when she discovered the joys of creating for children. "If my work touches a single mind or heart or funny bone, it has meaning," she says. "If it touches all three, it's magic!"

DORIAN CIRRONE is a former dance teacher, journalist, and instructor of English composition. Her poetry for adults has been accepted by several literary magazines. She says her poem "The Invitation" no doubt arose from the many misunderstandings she has encountered throughout life. She lives in south Florida with her husband and two children.

DAVE CRAWLEY is the "KD Country" feature reporter for KDKA-TV in Pittsburgh, Pennsylvania, where many of his stories appear in rhyme. His news reporting has won numerous awards, including six Mid-Atlantic Emmys. Dave began writing children's poems in 1996, and his work has appeared in *Jack and Jill*, *Cricket*, and *Spider* magazines. He credits his understanding of children to the fact that he never really grew up.

ELIZABETH DESCHRYVER is the manager of a technical writing group and has a Ph.D. in English. When she grows up, she wants to work in a museum, write children's books, and live in a tree house. Her favorite food is ice cream.

KATHY DUVAL writes, paints, and works as an art therapist in Houston, Texas. Her poem "Cosmic Cafe" was inspired by travels with her husband to west Texas, where spectacular sunsets and night skies brimming with stars are a visual feast.

JUDITH DYL lives with her husband in the foothills outside Tucson, Arizona. Now that her children are grown, she finally has time to watch the creatures that share her desert yard. She also swims, plays tennis, rides a bike, reads a lot of books, and writes stories and poems.

JILL ESBAUM lives with her husband and three teenagers on an Iowa farm (muddy brook and all). She loves taking ordinary subjects and twisting them into funny verses. "If I can make my own kids laugh, I know I have a winner," she says. "Sometimes they actually groan—they are WAY too honest!"

B. H. FIELDS is afflicted with a peculiar malady that compels him to write puns, limericks, and other low forms of humor. This renegade Ph.D. physicist left a twenty-five year career in industry and academe in 1996 to write full-time. He frequently pens a poem immediately upon arising, thereby going from bed to verse.

CLAUDIA HARRINGTON describes herself as a very tall writer living in southern California. "Did you ever sit behind a tall person at the movies and wish they'd take off their hat, only to discover they're not wearing one?" Her toes, by the way, *still* stick out of her bed (though she has yet to actually unscrew her head in order to fit better).

JASON HUNT runs the Renaissance Academy for the Arts and Sciences, a secondary school at which he and his wife, Cindy, teach everything from geometry to Latin. Jason and Cindy live with their three children, Angela, Alyssa, and Joshua, in Murfreesboro, Tennessee.

SUSAN MAREE JEAVONS is mother to eight children and grandmother to fifteen. Needless to say, she has plenty of inspiration for her writing. Susan has her own website, The Word Charmer's Web: www.suite101.com/myhome.cfm/the_word_charmers_web. She is also a contributing editor for Child Abuse & Recovery at Suite101.com, for which she writes biweekly articles on child-abuse awareness, prevention, and recovery.

ROXANNE KINNE is a full-time personal trainer at a small studio gym and also writes the gym's monthly newsletter. She enjoys children's poetry because it makes her laugh. The rest of her time is spent playing keyboard and singing in the praise band at her church. She is originally from Indiana, but now lives in California with a toothless calico cat named Vivian.

LISA HAGAN KLIEFOTH lives in Maryland with her husband, Chris, and their three children, Campbell, Willis, and Peyton, each of whom provides her with immense amounts of happiness and inspiration.

DENISE LONG wrote "The Human Pickle" for her sister, A.K., who, by all rights, should now be a Vlasic dill herself. Denise can't seem to stop herself from writing humorous poetry any more than her sister can stop eating pickles. "I take away all my pens and paper," she says, "but then I find one of those tiny mini-golf pencils and a half-blank scorecard and I'm at it again. . . ."

FONDA BELL MILLER, author of "Closet" and "Flee Flea," insists that she is not a funny person. She does, however, have a funny daughter, Emily, who has been known to organize in a disorganized way. Fonda also has a funny husband, a funny dog, two funny flealess cats, and a quite solemn hermit crab.

ANDREA PERRY is a children's poet who has had her work published in parents' magazines, children's magazines, Sunday school weeklies, and teaching journals. A member of the Society of Children's Book Writers and Illustrators, she lives with her husband and two children in Pittsburgh, Pennsylvania, and Jupiter, Florida. "Bedtime Prayer" was inspired by her son Dean, whose own bedtime prayers are often quite specific in nature.

TED SCHEU (pronounced "shy") is a writer and elementary school teacher in Middlebury, Vermont. He loves creating exuberantly humorous poems about his childhood in his own kid-voice—a voice he was much too shy to share at the time. And Max? Max was a genuine kid in one of Ted's classes, with a genuine locomotive mouth.

EILEEN SHERIDAN is a children's librarian at the Bridgeport (Connecticut) Public Library. She is also a volunteer at the Beardsley Zoo. Eileen's professional relationship with animals extends beyond the zoo, however; she reports that her writing is proofread by two cats and a guinea pig.

WENDI SILVANO has five children, a cat, and a dog. And a husband. She loves reading children's books, playing the piano, and eating banana cream pie. She has not spent too much time in "Time Out" lately . . . but some of her kids have.

PAT LORRAINE SIMONS feels as though she has already lived many lives. After getting married, she earned her degree, taught high school, retired, went to law school, raised two sons, practiced law, and retired again. In her current life, she is still married to her first husband and still has the same sons (now balding). She spends her time writing poetry, running a not-for-profit children's literacy organization in St. Louis, Missouri, and occasionally traveling to places where there are no telephone poles. "Zoops!" salutes Freddy and Faye, her fun-loving parents who taught her to play.

ROBERT ORA THOMAS lives in Westmont, Illinois, with his wife, Lynn, and their two sons, Keegan and Ayden. " 'Billy Bupper,' " Robert says, "just popped into my head one day while I was busy doing something else. Of course, I didn't have anything to write it down with at the time, so I had to repeat it in my head all day until I was able to locate a pen and paper. Ideas can be rude that way." As such, Robert has vowed never to have another one.

PENNY TRZYNKA writes poetry, stories, and health articles for children. She works as a school nurse, taking care of children in grades kindergarten through twelve, and credits her students with providing many of her writing ideas. She lives in Woodburn, Indiana, with her husband, two college-age daughters, a dalmatian, and a pet cockatiel.

SUZANNE WUNDER learned humor growing up in a family of nine brothers and sisters. Now that they all have their own children (twenty-four in all), her parents are doing all the laughing.

"Mouse House" © 2002 by Mary Ciotkowski
"The Invitation" © 2002 by Dorian Cirrone
"I Invited a Dragon to Dinner," "The Attic," and "Thoughts I Was Thinking While
 Drinking My Juice" © 2002 by Dave Crawley
"Catching Cold" and "Ice Cream on the Side" © 2002 by Elizabeth DeSchryver
"Cosmic Cafe" © 2002 by Kathy Duval
"Why Do I Have to Be Clean?" © 2002 by Judith M. Dyl
"A New View" © 2002 by Jill Esbaum
"The Man in the Green Hat That No One Can See" © 2002 by B. H. Fields
"Coming Unscrewed" © 2002 by Claudia Harrington
"Detestable Vegetables" © 2002 by Jason Hunt
"Another Rainy Day" © 2002 by Susan Maree Jeavons
"Sister Sally" © 2002 by Roxanne M. Kinne
"Martin's Extra Energy" © 2002 by Lisa Kliefoth
"The Human Pickle" © 2002 by Denise Long
"Closet" and "Flee Flea" © 2002 by Fonda Bell Miller
"Bedtime Prayer" © 2002 by Andrea Perry
"Maximillian's Mouth" © 2002 by Ted Scheu
"Show Time" and "The Tickle" © 2002 by Eileen Sheridan
"Time Out" © 2002 by Wendi Silvano
"Zoops!" © 2001 by Pat L. Simons, first published in the March 2001 issue of *Cricket* magazine
"Billy Bupper" © 2002 by Robert Ora Thomas
"Theodore Standitch" and "Under the Bed" © 2002 by Penny Trzynka
"My Mother Has Gone Crazy" © 2002 by Suzanne Wunder

Library of Congress Cataloging-in-Publication Data
I invited a dragon to dinner : and other poems to make you laugh out loud /
illustrated by Chris L. Demarest.   p. cm.
Summary: A collection of humorous poems about such subjects as pickles, dragons, and mothers.
1. Humorous poetry, American. 2. Children's poetry, American. [1. Humorous poetry.
2. American poetry—Collections.] I. Demarest, Chris L., ill. II. Philomel Books.
PS595.H8 P48 2002   [Fic] 811'.60809282—dc21 99-089398
ISBN 0-399-23567-1   10 9 8 7 6 5 4 3 2 1   First Impression